Salon Solutions

Salon Solutions

Salon marketing made easy without pulling your hair out

Susan Woodbury

A real salon owner who knows exactly what you're going through.

Library of Congress Control Number: 2009911652
ISBN: Hardcover   978-1-4415-9536-2
               Softcover   978-1-4415-9535-5

This book was printed in the United States of America.

To order additional copies of this book, contact:
Xlibris Corporation
1-888-795-4274
www.Xlibris.com
Orders@Xlibris.com
69697

I do wish to dedicate my book to all struggling hair salon owners who think there's no light at the end of the tunnel—and wish to give up. Stick with the goals you create by reading this book and your road to success will rise.

Special dedication to my husband Steven, who has always believed in me. I also wish to dedicate this book to my four month old grand-daughter, Symphony, who I hope one day, will be successful in the beauty industry.

A Little About Myself

As a business owner of ten years and only finally accomplishing things now (not because of lack of motivation, but lack of knowledge), I can relate to all you struggling owners who watch your staff sit around or take time off, while you continually work full time behind the chair, wondering why you decided to purchase (or start) the salon to begin with.

I decided to purchase my salon because all the salons I had ever worked for didn't care that you had a family. All they cared about was you be at their beckon call. One thing I'm about and will never compromise is that my family comes first. (Don't get me wrong. I'm a very dedicated and hard worker, but our families need us too).

I remember the day that I knew I was going to start my own business; I had no one on the books for this salon I was working at. I had been with this particular salon for about a year. My son was playing a soccer game only ten minutes down the road. I waited until my boss wasn't busy to ask if he minded if I shot down there for thirty minutes or so to watch my son play soccer, and his exact words "Well, hurry up!" I could tell he was agitated by his tone, and his rigid body language was so obvious. I did indeed go and watch my son play soccer, and I vowed to look into my own salon.

Do we really know what we're getting into when we purchase a business? Heck no! But lucky for you, now that I have the knowledge I have, you will know what you're getting into when purchasing your salon, or if you already own and need help asap, here I am.

First thing first, accountability. You have to be accountable to yourself about how your salon is running and how the staff operates. What do I mean by that? . . . You can't blame other people for how your salon is run on a daily basis. Employees don't know what's expected unless you tell them and put it in writing. One thing I've learned is people forget fast. Let me give

you an example if you're not quite sure what I'm talking about. Tell your staff about a promotion you're going to run at a staff meeting and see if they ever ask you about it again. I'll take bets on the answer being no. I once ran a Mother's Day promotion in-house and made some flyers up and posted them around the shop where clients could see them. At the end of the flyer, I let the recipients know that one lucky winner would be receiving free flowers if they took part in the promotion. We would keep track of who took advantage of the promotion and draw a lucky winner at the end of it. I held a few staff meetings and made sure the employees knew how the promotion worked. Guess what happened? Nothing, because the staff didn't talk about it and the clients didn't read the flyers. So in the end, I gave nothing away.

Start with taking a piece a paper and writing down things you would like to change about your salon and how you are going to achieve them. Don't worry if you don't know how to achieve them; that's why I wrote this book.

Being accountable for your salon also means you have to dig deep and truly accept what's happening. Don't make excuses for things you can control; you won't change it if you don't acknowledge it.

Side-note: The following are to get you thinking about each sentence and how you can change your salon. You can add your own ending to the sentence about your thoughts on it.

Ask yourself:

✂ If I could change one thing about my salon, it would be? (run more smoothly?)

✂ If I could change one thing about my own actions, it would be? (in tune to my staff more efficiently?)

✂ My salon could run better if I . . . ? (knew how to?)

✂ My short-term goal for the salon is (three months from now)? (be more team oriented?)

✂ If I could change my staff, it would be to . . . (get along better?)

✂ I need to work on myself about . . . (not getting so angry?)

Do You:

✂ Come in every day (on time) as a leader and role model for yourself and your staff? If you don't, you should!

- ✂ Hold staff meetings on a weekly basis? Employees need to know about work changes, promos, anything new, giving a positive to a team member who went the extra mile to help out.
- ✂ Meet with your staff to let them know if they're making their quota . . . meaning, are their numbers up?
- ✂ Curb any drama that might start in the salon?

Does:

- ✂ Your staff know what is expected of them, not only when they arrive to work, but throughout the day on downtime or if they are servicing a client?
- ✂ Your staff know how you want the clientele treated? Are you assuming they do or do you really know?
- ✂ Your salon have a policy manual in writing?
- ✂ Your salon have a procedure manual for every service you offer written and is it followed?

Do you:

- ✂ Teach your staff to up-sell on services and product?
- ✂ Make your staff accountable when something goes wrong?

✂ Tolerate backstabbing employees who can't get along to the point where you want to gouge your eyes out and call it quits?

Okay, that was a lot to start with, but don't be alarmed; we will take each area and break it down so you can be the person you want to be, and your salon can be one of the best-run salons around.

Ask yourself what kind of salon do you want to run? Do you party with your employees and try to be buddies with them rather than a boss? If you do, you're opening up a can of worms and not teaching your staff boundaries. Or, do you leave the salon most of the day and expect it to run smoothly with no systems in place so your staff members do what they want? Listen, you're not going to change anything, if you don't own up to things that need to be changed. If you're not the type of person to take control, then hire a manager or someone in your shop who can help. If you are the type who can take control, then good for you; but either way, you've got to own it, acknowledge it, so you can change it. If there wasn't an issue, you wouldn't be reading this manual.

Let's start with changing yourself. It could be one or two things, or it could be twenty. The important thing is taking one day at a time and implementing different strategies to make the changes you need. If you have a lot on the list, don't overwhelm yourself. You are not going to change things overnight; it just doesn't work that way. Chip away a little every day, and you will reap the rewards. Now come on, dig deep! You know those little things you could work on to change.

What have you written down for goals? You can't strive to achieve them if they're not written down. Start with short-term goals for yourself. It could be you don't want to work as much behind the chair or you want to make more money. The important thing is writing it down and figuring out how you are going to achieve it.

Next, write down goals for your salon and your staff . . . where do you see the salon in three months, six months, and one year? Don't make the goals so hard that you'll be disappointed when you don't reach them. Make them reasonable on something you think you can achieve. Make up a sheet, asking your employees what they would like changed in the salon or where they see themselves in six months. That way, when you meet with them, you'll have a better understanding about each of your employees.

Does the salon have a clear-cut manual that explains exactly to a tee what is expected of them? I mean from arriving to work on time, to how long lunch breaks are to be taken, to what is expected of them during downtime. There is nothing that should be left out. Take the time to jot down things that should be in the policy manual; this took me a while to write, but it has made my staff accountable to any arising issues. If employees have an issue with anything, I just simply go to my policy manual and show them what's written in it. Trust me, it saves so much energy and time. If you want to make sure it's legally correct in your state, then you could always have a labor-law lawyer go through it or call your local labor board to inquire.

Does the salon have a procedure manual to follow?
(Not a policy manual as stated above.)

That has been a Bible in my salon. For example, if you are waxing a client's eyebrows or lip, you (owner/manager) drape a towel over the client's chest so wax doesn't get on her blouse, but your employees do not and they accidentally get wax on the client's blouse . . . guess what? You just bought yourself a blouse. And now will that client ever return and how was that situation dealt with? How about a shampoo? Do you lather up and explain to your client what you're using and why? (If you're not, then you're not being a role model to your employees and you're losing a lot of money). How long does your shampoo last? Do you give a nice scalp massage for at least one to two minutes or are you

"zippity doo dah" and ten seconds is all they get? There's no right
or wrong way for you to run your salon as long as you make all of
your employees on the same page as you. But this is where that
accountability comes into play, and you have to ask yourself "How
do I want this salon run? How do I make the experience different
for my client? What makes me different than salons down the
road?" When you answer those questions, you will be in a whole
new ballpark. Also, remember that everything is trial and error;
if it doesn't work, then change it . . . as simple as that.

The reason you want your employees doing everything the same
way is to ensure you create "salon clients" and not "employee
clients." More about this later.

Your procedure manual should consist of everything you expect
from your employees. Every service you offer should be written
down how you want it performed and general questions should
be asked during every meeting you hold, with your employees, to
make sure they are following and know the manual. I consistently
watch my employees. It was tough in the beginning because
things take a while to catch on (remember the forgetfulness in the
beginning of the book?), and this is where accountability comes
into play. If they're not following your procedure manual, then
you need to pull them aside and talk to them about it. Ask them

why they are not following what is written. You need to do this, or there is no point in writing the manual.

If one of your other employees comes up to rat another employee out about not following the procedure manual or for anything else, then thank them and tell them you will start watching to make sure they are following it. Don't play too much into it; you don't want to start drama in your shop.

Also, make sure you allow your employees to help you write the manual, especially ones who have been with you for a long time. Remember it's new to, and it will go a lot smoother if they feel like you make them a part of something. If you're a new salon, then write it yourself, and your employees, once you hire them, will never know the difference.

Next thing is drama. How much do you have in your shop and how much do you play into it? Remember this is about accountability . . . being honest with yourself. If you're not, you will never change it. If you tend to get into the drama, then you will have to change that asap. You are the backbone and the leader to a group of people that will hopefully make you and themselves very successful someday. Does being part of any drama scene make you or them any money? No, so change it and move on. Now I won't just leave you hanging with "Oh my god, how am I going to change it?" It's a very simple system that I thought up one day and has worked well in my salon; in fact, when one of

 my girls is trying to create drama (because trust me, I don't have the perfect salon, just the right systems in place), the employee will simply ask the one trying to create the drama, "Problem or solution?" Yes, it really is that simple. You want to implement a problem-and-solution system in your shop. If one of your employees comes up and tells you something, first of all, did you need to know what the staff member is telling you; secondly, if you are getting into the drama before, here's a great way to change yourself immediately. Hold a staff meeting and tell them things are going to be changing. Start with making them accountable to themselves. Meaning, changing themselves on things they shouldn't be doing or talking about. If they're blaming other co-workers or even you, the boss, for things that they can change themselves, you need to sit with them and make them see differently. If there's a lot of drama in

the shop (which is usually a given until you know how to change it), then you tell them to constructively tell that co-worker what the issue is (so they can talk and work it out), and if they can't, you would be more than happy to help them through it. This is where problem and solution come in. When an employee comes to you for a problem, is it truly a problem or a chance for a dig with the co-worker not being able to hear it? For example, co-worker A tells co-worker C that co-worker B needs to clean better and how rotten they are at it. Now it's quite obvious that

co-worker A is trying to cause problems; this is where you need to train your staff that you will not tolerate this and they need to ask themselves, "If someone is telling me a problem about another co-worker or situation, are they looking for the solution or just being gossipy and drama (creating a problem)?" If they're not looking for a solution, then they (co-worker A) need to go and speak to that person and find the solution or go to the boss for help. You have to teach your staff about accountability and problem and solution to achieve the salon you know you want. Now not all staff members are going to work out and adjust to your new systems in place and you need to let them know that you will not tolerate it and written warnings will be handed out and, at times, employees will be sent home, and ultimately, it will cost them their job. I know it sounds scary with rising bills, but if you tolerate it now and don't change it, there's no point in owning this book. Throw it out and go back to the way you have been running your salon before.

Side-Note: Every state is different on how the firing process goes; make sure you call your labor board to get a copy or ask how the law works. You need to protect yourself from employees who think they have "one upped" you. Always know the laws and abide by them; that way, nothing can come back to bite you.

As things evolve the way you want, openly praise the employees you feel are doing a fabulous job and do it at the team meetings. It shows you've noticed and your expectations are what you say.

How much do you put into your salon?

This is always an interesting question when I talk to salon owners, because for some reasons, they think their staff should be working harder than they are. Yes, this is true to a point. But initially, when starting out or changing the way you run your existing or new salon, it's going to take time. Every time you change something for the better, you're one step to becoming the salon you want to be. Now, how much do you work behind the chair and how much do you promote the salon? If you work full time behind the chair, then how much time do you actually have to promote your staff? I'm a living, breathing person that can tell you I worked sixty plus hours a week and tried very hard to promote my staff, yet time and time again, I would

be doing all the work while they (the staff) waited for clients to not come through the door. Now, I'm going to tell you shortly, small things that don't cost a lot to market your salon, to not only get your staff busier so they can help pay the bills, but so you can cut back and work on your business, rather than in it.

Hopefully, by now, you have put or started to put a procedure manual and policy manual together, and you have curbed most of the drama and stuck to the accountability and the problem-and-solution system. If you're not, burn this book now and be done with it. You will never change a thing; I can only help people who want to change for the better. If you have started to put together a policy manual and procedure manual, great. It takes time, so make sure you stay on top of issues that arise and remember you're the leader. People follow by example, so be true

to yourself. I remember having the days of being behind the chair and trying to get the staff busy, and it's all on you—the pressure of everything coming down on you. I know, I will never forget being there and hoping there was a light at the end of the tunnel. Keep working on it . . . it will get better! Next thing is making sure everybody follows that procedure manual. You need to have meetings and everyone can role-play with each other to make sure they do greet, consult, shampoo, drape, offer the client a beverage, cutting techniques, blow-drying, hair setting, educating on products, etc. Whatever you offer, write a procedure on it. Trust me, I still add to mine today.

I'm serious on the role-playing. Employees will tell you they have read and understand the manual, but ask them to pretend you're a new client and greet you. How did they do? Probably nervous and out of sorts, but guess what? You Made Them Accountable . . . . Do that with every service periodically to ensure all staff members are on board.

If you have an employee that will not get on board with what you're trying to do, then you have a decision to make. It takes one bad egg to ruin the whole carton, and you need to decide if this person or these persons are holding you back to what you're trying to achieve. If you have someone like that and are willing to pull your hair out for them and continually try to mold them to your thinking and systems, then try it. But ask yourself how long you are going to deal with it before the ties are cut.

Before we move on, I want to touch base on how you price your services. This is where you might want to start thinking about having different prices in your salon. Are you the breadwinner right now? How many employees do you have and are they completely trained to your expectations? If they're not trained the way you do things yet, you can still offer different prices depending on how busy they are. So here's the goal. Once you have everyone on board to your liking, then you can go up on your (yes, you the owner/manager) prices and explain to your clients that your employees are trained under you and you're okay if they move down to one of them, should price become a problem. Explain you would like them (the client) to stay with the salon, and if they have any issues moving down to your qualified stylist, then you will be more than happy to show them (the stylist) the service to make sure it is completely duplicated. Make it all about your client so they feel very secure. You should have highly-trusted clients at this point, and if you've created or changed the way your salon is run, you should be golden. I know this is a lot of work, and you have enough on your plate with getting your staff where you want them to be, role-playing with procedures, and establishing a policy manual. But if you're going to move some of your clientele down to other stylists, then you need to make sure everyone in that salon cuts, razors, thins, chunks, etc., very similar. I know everyone styles differently, but the main part of the hair service should be similar. That will ensure your clients feel they get the same service with your stylist as they do with you. Have training days periodically to evaluate this. Clients love to be asked to be a model . . . who wouldn't? A free service will always make a client happy. And besides that, how different does that make your salon look? It shows you really care about your clients. Happy clients are repeat clients!

If you're just starting out and not established enough yet to achieve the tier pricing, you could always write it down for a future goal.

The way I run my price structure is as follows: I (the owner) have a three-tier price system that I put in place. I do not take on any new clients, so my prices aren't in this system; but yours could be, if you choose to. When a client calls based on pricing, we explain that we have a three-tier price system and our prices are based on how busy our stylists are and not by how good they are. All of our stylists go through a training process to ensure the clients get exactly what they want each and every time. We ask what the client is interested in, explain the prices, and ask if they have a preference on which one to go with. We ask for the booking. We do not wait for the client to ask for it. This has really worked great in the shop because when prices go up and that particular client doesn't want to pay that price, they go to a lower-priced stylist and not leave the shop all together. This is why it's so important that you create "salon" clients and not "employee" clients.

Side-Note: Being a leader, you know you are not above your employee's skill; you may have more experience, but that is knowledge you have to share and not knowledge that makes you think you're better than them. Your goal is to show them what you have so they may duplicate it and make them and the salon successful.

Have you ever noticed the amount of times you leave your client (who's paying you good money) to answer the phone and how nice are you really on the phone to the existing or new clients that are calling you to book an appointment or ask some questions? After all, who has time to talk on the phone when you left a dripping wet-headed client in the sink? I know it's an expense a lot of salons don't want to deal with, but trust me, your goal is to make yourself different and only a small percentage of salons have a receptionist. My receptionist is a godsend! She answers the phone professionally and has plenty of time to answer questions that the client might have without making them feel rushed and unimportant. She explains our prices to the client and asks what stylist pricing tier they would like to book with. She also asks them if they are looking for a drastic change with their hair or a trim. We get all of their personal information and put it into our computer system and note their new account about how they would like their hair done. That way, when the client comes in, the stylist already knows what the client would like and it's a nice ice-breaker for the relationship to start between them. It also sets the precedent that we really care about our clients. My receptionist also cleans, rebooks appointments, chats with clients while they are waiting, gets them a beverage, and makes sure the client is comfortable. Think of how annoyed you would be if a doctor had to keep leaving you, his patient, to answer the phone. Don't be worried if you can't afford one right now. Work it in your budget for the future, or better yet, see if a teenager or retired person who can fit into your shop will barter with you. Make sure they're trained to high expectations so your clients will be well taken care of, while you take care of the ones in your chair.

Should you have a contract?

Absolutely! I don't put a lot of work into my staff and in turn watch them leave and start their own salon. Be very picky who you choose to work for you, monitor them, and don't let them have access to everything in the salon. If you're an older salon, then, hopefully by now, you have already created loyal employees who watch out for their boss's well-being. They will in turn rat anyone out that would ever try to take phone numbers and addresses and walk out. And to be perfectly honest, if you don't have certain employees on board to what you are trying to create, then most likely they are the ones who would walk away with some clientele anyway.

This leads me to the next thing. I will show you in future chapters if that were to happen, how to get some of those clients back, but for right now, you need to create clients that are the "salon's" clients and not a certain "employee's" client. Now, we know we have those certain clients that will never leave that certain stylist. But if you create the right atmosphere, then whether that

employee leaves or not, you've created the atmosphere that the client loves. First thing is to make sure your staff mingle with all the clients. You can explain to your staff that if issues arise and a certain employee has to be out for a certain period of time, then one of your other staff members can accommodate that client. Think I'm kidding? I had three girls pregnant at the same time and due June, July, and August. We would rather see them go to a different staff member than to a different salon. Explain to your staff that as long as the client is spending their money with the salon, then so be it. I know we all have a little ego, but get over it and tell them to worry about future money they will make. Trust me, it works in my salon, and the staff have learned not to take it personal. Now, don't get me wrong; I'm very loyal to my staff and I would never let a client talk badly about any of them, but when the client lets me know they aren't happy with their last haircut (or whatever service they received), I suggest they try a different stylist in the salon. You would be amazed on how many clients are thrilled that we don't care. You have to train your salon like that . . . and remember it starts from the leader, so stick to your guns so we find a light at the end of that tunnel we're looking for. Remember, that's why every employee will be required to know that policy manual and perform it to a tee.

What kinds of marketing strategies do you have
in place to bring clientele in?

I hear you yelling at me, "I'm an owner, not a marketer." Stop
and take a deep breath. Marketing doesn't have to be about
spending thousands of dollars that you just don't have. If you're
a new salon owner with employees, then you can still use simple,
yet effective, flyers to bring in the clientele and in turn will be
able to work off those clients that come in by doing a referral
program. If you don't have the time or the inclination to pass out
the flyers yourself, then hire a teenager or someone that would

love to get their hair done for free. If they insist on getting paid, then you could give them a small percentage of the amount of people that come in off the flyers.

What to put in the flyer?

Ask yourself, "Who do I want to market to? What type of clients?" Do you like to promote perms, cuts, colors, foils, etc? Don't say you want to market to everyone because that just doesn't work. You have to pick your target market and work off that. Now, that doesn't mean on your next flyer that you won't target other types of people. Just know that each time you work on a marketing campaign, ask yourself who you want to target. Second thing, flyers don't have to be pretty and glossy. They can be a plain-Jane flyer as long as you capture your target audience's attention. Third thing, offer an irresistible deal. You can call it anything you want. Who's in for stars right now that everyone wants to look like or be like? You can call it that package. FYI: You don't want to offer the "Jennifer Lopez" package if your flyer is geared toward perms.

Make sure it makes sense to people. If it doesn't make sense, you didn't capture their (the prospective clients) attention, and the whole thing will be a waste of time, money, and energy. The headline will be the attention getter. Some of the best headlines that grab attention are as follows:

- Who else wants (fill in the blank). You could use, "to look like _____."
- The secret of (fill in the blank). Could be makeup or a hair color.
- Little known ways to (fill in the blank).
- Get rid of (problem, fill in the blank).
- Here's a quick way to (solve the problem, fill in the blank).
- Now you can have (something desirable, fill in the blank).
- Do something like (pick someone famous that everyone can relate to, fill in the blank).
- What everyone should know about (big curiosity, makes readers want to see if they're missing something, fill in the blank).

Play around with different ways to start your flyer. It takes time to get the hang of it, but the important thing is to not give up and remember, it's all trial and error. If something doesn't work, don't do it again. If it creates awesome results, do it again when you have slow times to fill in the gaps.

Now the body of the flyer should go with the headline. If you said "Who else wants to look like (someone who is popular) for a fraction of the cost. "Introducing: The Jennifer Lopez Glamour Package".

What to offer?

People like good deals. It doesn't matter if it costs you pennies or not. To the clients, if it's a good deal, they will buy, but only if they are in the market to buy what you are selling. It doesn't matter if you're giving hair colors away for free. If a bald man reads or skims that flyer, it's obvious you probably won't get him for a client. That's what target marketing applies to. We obviously didn't want to target bald men.

Before we move on to what you will put in your package deal (or whatever you have named it), you need to understand how to price things in your shop. What do you give away for free in your salon now? Do you give free hand massages while the client sits under the dryer or do you give away eyebrow waxes? Whatever you do for services needs to have a price put on it. Why? Because if there's no price on it, there's no value on it. If you're giving an eyebrow wax for free, you need to put a price on it. Let's use $10. Now the client knows they're getting an eyebrow wax valued at ten dollars for free. That means more to a client than just giving something with no value on it for free. Let's take a scalp massage and put a value on it. I know you're probably screaming, "I don't do scalp massages," but yes, you do. When a client gets a shampoo and condition at the shampoo bowl, do you not massage their head? Let's say you normally shampoo and condition for a total of one to two minutes. Let's add on an extra one or two minutes, and voila, you got yourself a scalp massage. But ah ah ah, don't forget to put a value on it. We'll say $20. I know this might get confusing, but you need to put a value on everything you do in your salon so the packages you create will work for you.

Once you have value on everything, it will be a lot easier for you to create your packages. The more things you have in your salon to put a value on, the better you will be when creating different packages. Some of the things we have in my salon are:

- ✂ Eye, lip, chin waxing ($12 each)
- ✂ Polish change ($15)
- ✂ Color gloss (adds shine in the hair and last eight to ten shampoos) ($30)
- ✂ Deep-conditioning treatment ($25)
- ✂ Scalp massage ($20)
- ✂ Makeup application ($30-$45)
- ✂ Free product that my reps have given me (approx $20 value)
- ✂ Charging per foil ($3-$6, depending on what stylist you get)
- ✂ Tan session ($8)

By putting a value on each of these services that don't cost me diddly-squat, I've allowed my clients to feel they're getting something of value for free. So when you're putting your package together, make sure the headline, the name, and the package all flow together. We'll say you geared your headline and package name for a color and cut. You can do something like this:

Call now (this tells the client what you want them to do) and book for your (name of package) and get a sexy new color and cut, valued at $_____, and receive absolutely free: waxing (valued at), scalp massage (valued at), color gloss (valued at), and so on. By putting a value on things that doesn't cost the salon much, you planted the seed in your clients' heads that they get all this great stuff for free. Now I hear you saying, "But am I ripping my clients off?" Listen, if you're being dishonest, using crappy products, and not making the experience and the service about your client, then yes, you're being dishonest to them. But if you are using quality products and really making the experience about your client, then no, you're not ripping your client off. You're only creating a great package for them, but you're also making their experience one they will remember.

Now you need to remember to track all of this. First, how much did the flyers, ads, or however you promoted this campaign cost? Secondly, you need to track each client you get from the promotion and what they spent. That way, you can tell if it is worth doing and if you'll do it again. Hope that makes sense.

Now that everything has a price (value) on it, this is where you can up-sell to create more revenue for your salon and your employees. As an example, a color gloss, as stated above, costs $30 to a client coming in for this service. A color-gloss tube costs the salon approx $10 and can get an abundance of applications. We offer all of our clients who get a hair service a deal of $10 instead of $30—that's called up-selling. Now you've added ten additional dollars to the employees' work total. Every time a client gets a hair service, the employee is instructed to ask the client if they would like a color gloss normally going for thirty dollars for ten dollars. They tell the client what the benefits of the product are and why they should get the gloss. If each stylist up-sells ten per week, that's an additional $100 in revenue per stylist per week!

Okay, how else can you market to your clients?

Are you on a busy road or have a lot of traffic going by each day? If you do, then you need a sandwich board outside. It's double sided, so you can put two separate things on it. Remember when doing promotions on it to be different. Don't just put "For the best service in town, try us." Blah, Blah, Blah. Do you have the best service? And if you do, why? Do you offer something the salon down the road doesn't? You need to make yourself different than any other salon. When you've done that, you're on the right track to success. Change the sign bi-weekly or monthly to ensure your clients will keep reading it. Don't discount, add value. Remember the package deals?

Referral program. How do you thank the client that sent you in someone new to your salon? Do you just simply say "Thank you," or do you send them a thank-you letter with a coupon to use on their next visit? Now don't be cheap and send them a $5-off coupon on their next visit. What is five lousy dollars? Come on! Be different. In my salon, we give all referrals 20 percent off to use on their next visit. Why? Because think about how much your new client will bring in for revenue over a years' time. A lot more than giving twenty percent off to the person who referred the new client and because we give a decent percentage off, we get a lot more referrals. Take excellent care of your clients, and you'll have repeat ones forever.

Side-Note: If your staff knows the client is coming in and getting 20 percent off, this is where they need to up-sell to that client. It could be adding on a color gloss for shiny hair, a wax, or something that will offset that discount. You don't have to do a percentage off for referrals, you can think of your own special referral program. Don't make it product unless your rep is giving you a deal. You don't want to cut into product profits. In January and February, I did an awesome referral program. Whoever sent in a new person for any service (not to buy products) got exactly back, on a gift card, whatever the new client spent. Now, I know you've quit breathing for a minute thinking how crazy something like that is, but remember, it made me different and when it should have been a dead time of year unless I did some heavy advertising (which I did not), we were crazy busy. I'm not kidding you; clients who have been with us for years and never referred anyone were sending in two or three clients at a time. I will definitely do that every year. Now, the staff knew we were doing this and the way the free service to the clients that had referred someone new in worked was the staff had to do the service for free and up-sell a service to create more revenue for themselves. Also educating the client on product would hopefully ensure that they would buy. Every salon is different. You do what works for your salon.

Do you have a website? I'm telling you, in this day and age, you need one and you need to advertise that you have one on every piece of advertisement you send out. It took me approximately five to six months to build my own, but it came out great. It has made us different, and we've gotten a lot of business from it. If you have the money and want someone else to build it, then so be it. But remember, glamorous and pretty sell nothing. You have to make yourself different. If you want to build your own using salon templates, then research it, and you'll find many to choose from online. Go on to different ones and jot down what you don't want on yours and what you do. Remember, be Different. I can't emphasize that enough.

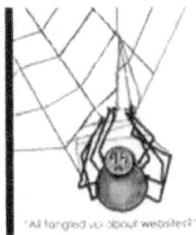

"All tangled up about websites?"

Monthly package deals. Hopefully by now, you've figured out how the packaging deals work and it's up to you and your staff to get creative with who you should be targeting to and what you want to offer and to create demand and scarcity (meaning limit the amount so clients think if they don't get on board now, then they'll lose out). I went online and printed a calendar of holidays and created packages for the different holiday seasons. Be creative and let your staff help with ideas. You might have some other events in your area that you can gain some exposure for your salon. Make each package a little different. You don't want to run the same exact packages with a different name. Clients will see right through that. Look at your list of services you offer and what you're up-selling (things that don't cost you a lot) and do monthly packages in advance. You don't want to be running a package for May and starting in May. You need to start three to four weeks in advance and get the word out by using flyers, outside billboard, and promoting on your Web site, hanging posters in your shop, making sure your employees are on board with what's going on, and using your answering machine to promote upcoming events.

Hopefully, you have a computer to keep track of all your clientele. If you don't, this could take a lot of time, but it's worth it. Have you ever wondered what happened to all those clients that never come back? Well, we're going to "wake the dead" and see who we can bring back in. What I mean is every three months, you're going to look for the clients that haven't been in for at least three to four months and write to them. You're going to offer them a ten-dollar-off coupon to come back and get a service from the salon. Once you send the first letter with the coupon (set to expire in six weeks), then a second letter will go out in three weeks for those who have not come back from the first letter. You'll be surprised at how many come back after the second letter as opposed to the first. My rate on these letters can have a return from 75 percent to 90 percent. It's amazing what motivates people. I have yet to figure it out! Now you don't have to write to the "Pitas." What? I know you have them; everyone does. We shorten it for "Pain In The Ass!" We have a computer, and if we don't want to write to someone, because we don't want them back, then we simply hyphenate their first name and put, for example, Susan-pita; that way, we remember not to ever try to get them back.

Next, how do you fill last-minute gaps and cancellations? I know you have them; everyone does. You walk in and see large holes in your books and wonder how the hell you are going to make the rent, pay the bills, and find the light at the end of the tunnel. Well, you're going to sign up to text your customers for last-minute appointments, and you're going to e-mail your clients. Each of these services can be found on the Internet. Don't go with the first one you see. Make sure the price is fair, and you can easily navigate the site. Think about what using these services does for you and your clients. First, it gets your open gaps busy, so the salon is producing and the staff is busy. And secondly, it keeps your clients attached right at your hip where they belong. How many salons do you know that stay attached to their clients like that? Not many. Now you don't have to use these two services for just dead days. You can e-mail monthly newsletters to let your clients know what's going on in the shop or have an employee tell them a little about themselves, which keeps it more personal.

If you are computerized, keep track of birthdays and anniversaries. My salon prints out a weekly list and sends a $10-off coupon that never expires. You would be surprised to see the clients you haven't seen in a while coming back.

Pick a business of the month and offer a sweet deal. That helps fill empty holes in the day and makes a business feel really special. Think of all the repeat clients you could get from that.

All new clients receive a handwritten note from their stylists thanking them for coming in and personalizing it with something they chatted about. I read each and every one before they get sent.

I send a thank-you letter from the salon to all new clients and give them a ten-dollar voucher for them to use on their next visit and another to give to a friend, friend, or co-worker. I will set those vouchers to expire in six weeks.

All new clients get a complimentary color gloss and paraffin dip on their first visit. This makes them feel really special! Remember we put a value on these services; so the clients know they are getting $50 in services for free.

For employees that leave the salon, make a list of their clients and send a sweet deal for them to enjoy. Track the ones you keep and send a series of three letters to the ones who haven't come back. You will be surprised at how many will stay with you if you create "salon" clients and not "employee" clients.

With all these marketing strategies that don't cost much to run, you can be well on your way to big profits, less stress for you, more time for you, and a well-run salon, which is almost unheard of today.

At this point, you should, if you have followed what is given to you for knowledge in the beginning of this guidebook, have all the ammunition to run your salon to the fullest—starting with the accountability to not only yourself, but also making your employees accountable to the way they are and how the salon is run. Hopefully, you are using the problem-and-solution system, which ties into the accountability of making people aware of what they're trying to create when they talk about other staff members. You should have your price levels in place, or however you choose to do them, and know how to put a value on everything you do in the shop and teach the staff how to up-sell. You should have purchased a yearly calendar as well as known all holidays and events in your area. You should have on each month in your calendar what you will be running for packages, events, or specials, and you should know how you're going to get the word out to promote them. You should have a policy manual in place as to what is expected of your employees and consequences when the policy isn't followed. You should also have your procedure manual in place for every service you do in the shop. You want each one to be written exactly how you want it performed. Weekly staff meetings are important to keep your team on the same page. Offer positive feedback when you see an employee do something, and if you need to bring up "needs work" with something in the shop, then so be it. Let your staff be part of it, and let them speak about things that are important to them. You set the precedent, but make sure they know they're important to you. Never embarrass an employee. If they need to be spoken to about something big, then save that for you and that staff member. Numbers need to be looked at for each employee and the salon itself. I run my numbers weekly to make sure they're up and to see what staff member is down. I do bring those up at the meetings because the staff

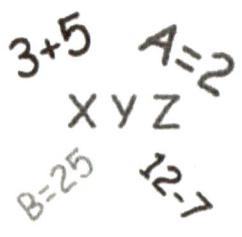

members know those numbers keep the business going. Every three months, I run everyone's numbers and meet with them to let them know how they're doing and what I need them to improve on.

Hopefully, you give ten percent to your staff on retail sales. I do! I have each staff member pick a month and give out their checks yearly. I do, however, keep track of their retail sales, weekly. I expect 10 percent of their service sales to be in retail. I don't mind 15 percent, but I would love each staff member to do 20 percent of their service sales in retail. For example, if Jessica does $1000 a week, I expect her retail sales to be at least $100. Again, I will accept ten percent, but would love twenty.

Have you made yourself accountable for things you can change? Ask yourself the following questions:

Have you implemented a policy manual?

Have you implemented a procedure manual?

How is your salon running over-all?

Have you written your future goals down?

Have you met some of your goals?

Have you seen a difference in your employees using accountability and problem/solution?

Do you role-play to make sure everyone's on board?

Have you implemented hair-training sessions with your staff?

Do you have a tier-price system?

Have you hired a manager or realized you are the ultimate role model? (It starts from the top)

Do you run meetings on a weekly basis?

Do you run your numbers on a weekly basis?

Does your staff know where their numbers are?

Have you implemented value-packaging offers?

What are you doing for marketing?

Do you have a marketing calendar?

Do you continually market for the next month?

By reading this book, I hope you will be able to answer the questions at the beginning of the book and now, with the knowledge you've gained, have short-and long-term goals for you and your staff. Remember, everything is trial and error. If it works, continue to use it. If it flops, then get rid of the promotion.

I wish you many years of success with your salon.